undercover operations

Adam
Sutherland

Lerner Publications Company
Minneapolis

Lerner Publications Company
A division of Lerner Publishing Group, Inc.
241 First Avenue North
Minneapolis, MN U.S.A.

Website address: www.lernerbooks.com

Library of Congress Cataloging-in-Publication Data

Sutherland, Adam.
    Undercover operations / by Adam Sutherland.
      p.   cm. — (On the radar: Defend and protect)
    Includes index.
    ISBN 978-0-7613-7773-3 (lib. bdg. : alk. paper)
    1. Intelligence service—Juvenile literature.
    2. Undercover operations—Juvenile literature.
    3. Espionage—Juvenile literature. I. Title.
JF1525.I6S89 2012
327.12—dc23   2011031684

Manufactured in the United States of America
  – CG – 12/31/11

Acknowledgments: Alamy: Photos 20, 25; Dreamstime:
Basphoto 2tl, 10–11, Hypestock 3br, 19b, Nicemonkey
24–25; Getty Images: cover, 9; iStock: Andrew J Shearer
21, Vika Valter 16–17; Shutterstock: Ryan Rodrick Beiler
4–5, Anthony Correia 15l, Fred Goldstein 12–13, Kheng
Guan Toh 30–31, K2 Images 12br, Peter Kim 6br, Martin
Muránsky 2tr, 18tr, P Cruciatti 18br, Rorem 7tr, Martin Spurny
, Testing 15r, Jurgen Ziewe 19tr; Wikimedia: 2br, 8, 13c, 14l,
4r, 26, 26–27, 28c.

Main body text set in
Helvetica Neue LT Std 13/15.5.
Typeface provided by Adobe Systems.

cover stories

CONTENTS

the**people**

the**skills**

the**talk**

Protect and serve

The U.S. Secret Service's main mission is to protect the country against financial and computer fraud. (Money laundering, for example, is an important source of funds for many terrorist organizations.) The Secret Service also protects the U.S. president both at home and on foreign visits.

Members of the Secret Service were on duty during Barack Obama's swearing in as president in 2009.

TOP SECRET AGENCIES

Surveillance and intelligence gathering are both types of undercover operations carried out by specialized government agencies. The agencies are often referred to as secret services, because their duties are not well known.

ACTING ON INTELLIGENCE

In the United States, the Central Intelligence Agency (CIA) collects information about foreign governments, companies, or individuals and passes that information to the U.S. government. The CIA also conducts undercover operations and military missions.

DEFENDING THE UNITED STATES

The main goal of the Federal Bureau of Investigation (FBI) is to protect and defend the United States against terrorist and foreign intelligence threats and to uphold and enforce criminal laws. The FBI is increasingly involved in protecting important computer systems against cyber attacks.

BRITISH SECURITY SECTIONS

The British Security Service, also known as Military Intelligence, Section 5 (MI5), is responsible for protecting its country against threats to national security. MI5 guards Britain against espionage attempts from other countries, terrorism, and sabotage. The Secret Intelligence Service (SIS), or Military Intelligence, Section 6 (MI6), collects Britain's foreign intelligence. It finds information on the plans of foreign governments or terrorist groups and disrupts their activities.

SPYCHATTER

Break the spy speak code with
On the Radar's stealthy guide!

code name
a secret name that is designed
to protect a person's identity

homeland security
efforts to prevent a terrorist
attack on home soil

sabotage
the deliberate destruction
or damage of something

counter-intelligence
activities designed to stop or
attempt to stop enemy spying

informer
someone who provides
information, usually top secret

surveillance
closely watching a person
or a group of people

counter-narcotics
operations to prevent the
growing, transportation,
and selling of drugs

intelligence
information gathered
by undercover agents

undercover
acting in secret

national security
the safety of a country

wiretapping
secretly connecting to a
telephone line to listen
to conversations

counter-terrorism
the methods that governments
use to prevent terrorist threats
and attacks

electronic surveillance
using hidden microphones to
secretly monitor conversations

espionage
spying

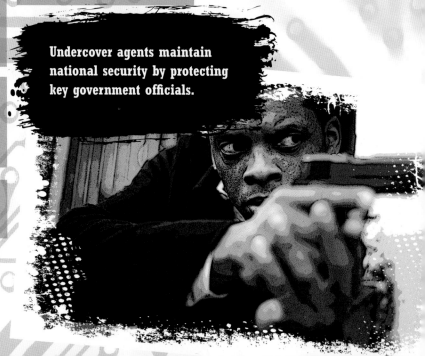

Undercover agents maintain
national security by protecting
key government officials.

GLOSSARY

assassination
the organized killing
of someone

cipher
a secret or disguised way
of writing; a code

computer fraud
using computers to obtain
information and using it to
commit a crime

cyber attacks
the use of computer viruses
to disrupt or crash a
computer system

disloyal
not faithful or loyal, not
trustworthy

enslaved
made to work as a slave

fictional
made up, not real

hieroglyphs
an ancient Egyptian form
of writing with pictures

identity
a person's name, address,
and personal history

money laundering
a way of disguising where
money from criminal activities,
such as drug dealing, has
come from

overthrow
the removal or downfall
of a country's leader

political assassinations
killings done for
political purposes

political tensions
arguments between groups
with different political views

recruited
persuaded to join
an organization

regain
to take or win back something

satellite
a device in space that orbits
Earth, taking photographs or
sending information as radio
signals

THE STORY OF ESPIONAGE

Espionage, or spying, has been going on for thousands of years. As far back as 500 B.C., ancient Chinese military leaders wrote detailed studies on how to trick their enemies. Hieroglyphs show spies operating in the ancient Egyptian court. Spies were used to uncover disloyal subjects and to locate groups that could be taken over and enslaved.

Sir Francis Walsingham (1532–1590) was one of Queen Elizabeth I's most trusted advisers—and a legendary English spy.

ROMAN INTELLIGENCE

The Roman Empire's intelligence forces provided reports on the military strength of its enemies. The Roman military hired spies to become members of rebel tribes and convince leaders to join forces with Rome. In 44 B.C., Roman spies told Julius Caesar of the plot to kill him, but he chose to ignore the information and was killed by his enemies.

SPYING THROUGH THE AGES

In the sixteenth century, the English royal court developed the world's leading spy network. King Henry VIII created a large secret police force. He used it to locate groups loyal to the Roman Catholic Church, which he was trying to eliminate in England. His daughter, Elizabeth I, employed at least 50 secret agents in England and across Europe to discover plots to overthrow her.

REVOLUTIONARY ACTS

George Washington and Benjamin Franklin both spied against the British during the Revolutionary War (1775–1783). Washington was an expert in military trickery. He once tricked the British Army into believing he was about to attack New York City when his troops were actually in Yorktown, Virginia, nearly 400 miles (640 kilometers) away!

EAST VERSUS WEST

After World War II (1939–1945), political tensions arose between the United States and its allies and the Soviet Union and China. These tensions provoked an intense period of spying known as the Cold War (1945–1991). This conflict saw a massive expansion in nuclear weapons building. Both sides hired spies to uncover the enemy's secrets.

CIA director Leon Panetta *(front right)* and his key aides informed Congress in person that Osama bin Laden had been killed.

Spying on terrorists

In the last 20 years, agencies have been more likely to target the illegal drug trade and the threat of terrorism than spy on age-old enemies. The discovery of Osama bin Laden's hideout and information leading to the SEAL Team Six raid is believed to have been supplied by CIA informers.

KEEPING MY COUNTRY SAFE

MY STORY BY "ALEX"

From an early age, I had always been drawn to the idea of working in intelligence. But I never really knew how to go about getting into this field.

After graduating from college with a degree in history and politics, I went to a job fair to see what kind of opportunities were available for someone with my degree. While there, I spoke with some people who were recruiting for the CIA. I decided to apply.

The application process was hard. I was put through physical, psychological, and polygraph tests. Almost a year later, I had the job. But I still had to go through an intensive six-month training program.

After training, I joined a small team working on counternarcotics. There was a real sense of achievement among us when things went according to plan. We all wanted our colleagues to succeed in gathering secret intelligence and to return safely from their missions.

After that, I spent a couple of years in Afghanistan. I worked closely with the U.S. military and various partners on counterterrorism operations. This was definitely an experience of a lifetime.

On my return to Washington, D.C., I began working on terrorist threats to U.S. interests. I work closely with the CIA's Directorate of Intelligence and the police to stop the threats from becoming a terrorist attack. As a person with family members who were working near the World Trade Center on September 11, 2011, it isn't hard to be inspired to come to work each day. Part of my role is to try to ensure that the intelligence we get will stop a terrorist plot.

Working for the CIA, you really do feel that you are making a difference. I regularly have moments where I stop and think, "I can't believe that I'm actually being paid to do this." Not a lot of people can say that!

THE CIA

Like every secret service, the CIA has its own unique structure. This is how the U.S. intelligence agency is organized to fight terrorism and to keep the United States safe.

ACTING ON INTELLIGENCE

Officers in the CIA's Directorate of Intelligence (DI) are expected to track fast-moving international developments and decide what effect they will have on the United States. DI officers produce reports such as the daily World Intelligence Review (WIRe). The WIRe is an electronic publication aimed at senior U.S. government officials. The CIA analysis of overseas intelligence helps to keep the government well informed of events that are going on around the world.

VERY IMPORTANT PEOPLE

The job of Human Resources (HR) is to hire the brightest talent and to help them develop the skills needed to serve their country. The CIA's recruitment center is constantly looking to hire highly qualified men and women from a wide range of ethnic and cultural backgrounds. It has struck up partnerships with several U.S. colleges and universities that are important sources of talent.

The Office of Public Affairs (OPA) made sure that President Obama was fully briefed before he told the nation that the mission to find Osama bin Laden had been successful.

UNDERCOVER OPERATIONS

The National Clandestine Service (NCS) is the CIA's undercover arm. It coordinates and monitors undercover operations across all the U.S. intelligence agencies. With the aim of strengthening national security, the NCS collects information from its contacts around the world and briefs the president and senior government officials on important discoveries.

INFORMING THE PUBLIC

The CIA communicates with the outside world through the OPA. The OPA director oversees all the CIA's dealings with the press, television, radio, and the public. While always protecting classified information, the OPA has made a large amount of information about the agency available to the public to try to provide openness and to encourage trust among U.S. citizens.

TECHNICAL SUPPORT

The Directorate of Science and Technology (DS&T) creates the NCS computer systems and data analysis programs. Workers come from fields such as computer programming and engineering. They bring a range of different skills to the job, from code breaking to designing new satellite surveillance techniques.

GLOBAL INTELLIGENCE

Undercover operations and intelligence gathering are crucial parts of every nation's security planning. This means that each country has its own well-organized and well-funded secret service. Here are some of the best known.

Like the CIA and many other secret services, the BND and SVR have their own symbols *(left and above).*

GERMAN PROTECTION

Germany's foreign intelligence agency is the Bundesnachrichtendienst (BND, or Federal Intelligence Service). It acts as an early warning system to alert the German government to threats from abroad. Using wiretapping and electronic surveillance, the BND collects information on threats such as terrorism and organized crime. With 300 offices in Germany and around the world, the BND employs about 6,000 people (10 percent are trained soldiers).

RUSSIAN SECURITY

The Russian Foreign Intelligence Service (SVR) is responsible for intelligence and espionage activities outside Russia. It advises the Russian president on security threats from abroad. It is authorized to negotiate antiterrorist cooperation and intelligence-sharing arrangements with foreign agencies. Until 1991 the SVR was part of a larger secret police called the

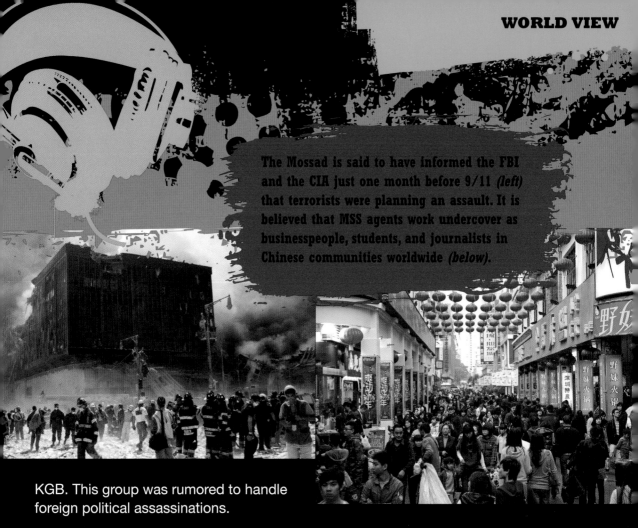

The Mossad is said to have informed the FBI and the CIA just one month before 9/11 *(left)* that terrorists were planning an assault. It is believed that MSS agents work undercover as businesspeople, students, and journalists in Chinese communities worldwide *(below)*.

KGB. This group was rumored to handle foreign political assassinations.

FRANCE FIGHTS TERRORISM

The General Directorate for External Security (DGSE) is France's external intelligence agency. The agency works alongside the Central Directorate of Interior Intelligence to provide information and protect national security through counterintelligence operations abroad. The DGSE may have prevented more than 15 terrorist attacks in France since 9/11.

ISRAELI OPS

The Mossad is Israel's national intelligence agency and is responsible for information gathering and undercover operations outside Israel's borders. Together with Aman (military intelligence)

and Shin Bet (internal security), the Mossad makes up a vital part of Israel's intelligence network and community.

EASTERN INTELLIGENCE

The Ministry of State Security (MSS) is China's largest and most active foreign intelligence agency. One of its main roles is gathering foreign intelligence. Its agents are active all over the world. The Chinese government seeks intelligence from all parts of Chinese life, so employees are active in many areas including politics, business, industry, and education.

15

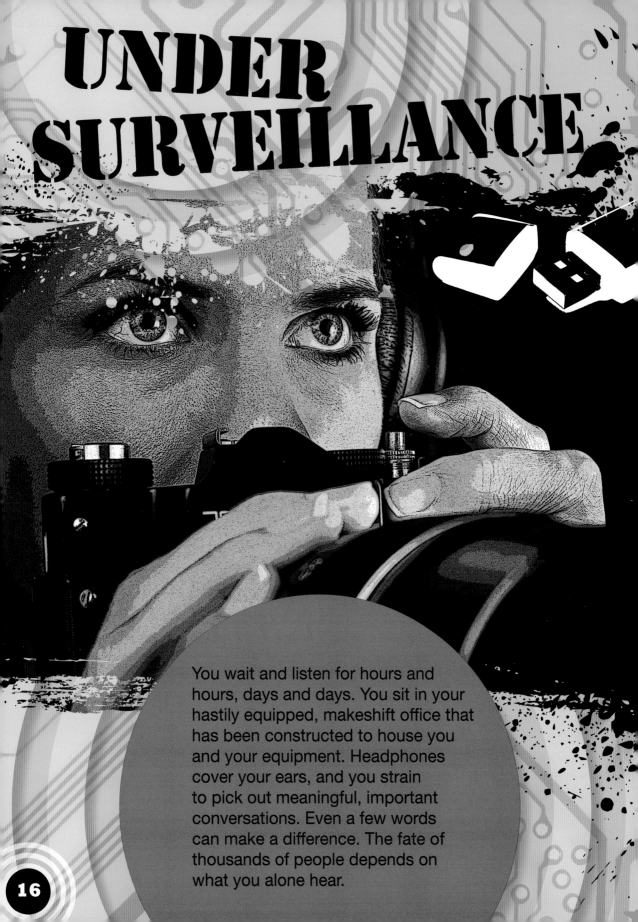

UNDER SURVEILLANCE

You wait and listen for hours and hours, days and days. You sit in your hastily equipped, makeshift office that has been constructed to house you and your equipment. Headphones cover your ears, and you strain to pick out meaningful, important conversations. Even a few words can make a difference. The fate of thousands of people depends on what you alone hear.

ON WATCH

You've been tracking this target for months. All the intelligence points to him being linked with a group of extremists who are thought to be planning terrorist attacks. It is your team's job to locate him, track his movements, and find a way of monitoring who he talks to and what he says.

COLLECTING EVIDENCE

The biggest challenge is getting a listening device into position. Terrorists know their cell phones can be used to track their location and monitor their conversations. But some terrorists are more careful than others. You discovered their headquarters three months ago, thanks to a conversation between two younger recruits to the group. After that, it was a case of figuring out how to get a microphone in there. But you did it and it's proving invaluable.

READY TO ACT!

Suddenly you hear something important. Your heart starts to thud like a drum as you realize the significance of the words. The hairs on the back of your neck stand up, but you must stay calm. This could be the breakthrough you've been waiting for— the chance to pass this information back to headquarters and let them plan the next move. You could be the key to putting these terrorists behind bars! You feel exhilarated and a small thrill rips through you like a jolt of electricity. You feel proud to be keeping your country safe.

YOU ARE NOT ALONE!

Undercover organizations have developed several clever ways to track their targets. Here are their key spying techniques.

WATCHING THE WEB

Organizations such as the FBI spend millions of dollars monitoring Internet traffic. People who visit certain websites or use particular trigger words can be picked out by computer programs and flagged for closer review.

STREET CORNER CAMERAS

The installation of Closed-Circuit TV (CCTV) is common in Britain. Its use in the United States and Canada is growing rapidly.

SOCIAL SPY NETWORKS

The information that suspected criminals leave on social networking sites such as Facebook and Twitter can be used to extract useful information about them.

EYES IN THE SKY

The United States uses unmanned aerial vehicles (UAVs) to patrol the U.S.-Mexican border. The UAVs are watching for illegal immigrants.

CELL PHONES

The FBI pays two of the largest phone companies—AT&T and Verizon—over a million dollars every year to be able to search the records of all the phone calls made on their lines.

CCTV is used for general security and for traffic offenses, but it is also increasingly used for surveillance by undercover organizations.

Some governments in the world are allowed to monitor all Internet activity.

UAV cameras are so sensitive that they can sense the heat of a human body from 37 miles (60 km) away.

Most cell phone surveillance is used to track the whereabouts of the phone user.

19

JAMES BOND

THE ULTIMATE SPY

THE BIRTH OF 007

James Bond first hit the spy scene in 1952, when writer Ian Fleming created the character. James's father, Andrew, was Scottish. His mother, Monique Delacroix, was Swiss. The young Bond spent his childhood traveling around Europe because of his father's work in the arms industry. As a result, James Bond speaks French and German fluently.

GROWING UP FAST

When James was just 11 years old, his parents were killed in a mountain climbing accident. He moved back to England to live with an aunt, Miss Charmaine Bond. He went to Eton College, one of Britain's most prestigious private schools but was expelled for bad behavior!

After college, Bond joined the Royal Navy, rising to the rank of commander.

SECRET SERVICE

While in the navy, Bond joined the Special Boat Service (SBS), Britain's elite special operations group. From the SBS, Bond was recruited by the Royal Naval Reserve (RNR) Defence Intelligence Group. He studied Asian languages and won high grades for physical endurance, logic, and psychological operations. He joined MI6 at the age of 30.

LICENCE TO KILL

The two zeroes in Bond's code name 007 refer to the two kills he made in the book, *Casino Royale,* to join the ranks of the senior MI6 agents. Bond favors the Walther PPK pistol, although he is also an expert of close-quarters combat and martial arts. He drives an Aston Martin DB5. When he is not on assignment, he lives in an apartment in Chelsea, London, and says his favorite food is scrambled eggs. An ordinary man with an extraordinary job, James Bond is the most famous secret agent in history!

Career highlights

1953 first Bond novel, *Casino Royale*, is published

1962 first Bond film, *Dr. No*, is released with actor Sean Connery playing James Bond

2006 original Aston Martin DB5 is sold for $4.2 million

2012 23rd Bond film, as yet untitled, is scheduled for release on November 9, 2012

THE STATS

Name: James Bond
Created: 1952
Place of birth: Scotland
Height: 6 feet (2 meters)
Weight: 167 pounds
(76 kilograms)
Job: Intelligence officer
for Britain's MI6

Daniel Craig took over the role of James Bond in 2006 in the film *Casino Royale* followed by *Quantum of Solace* in 2008.

INVISIBLE INK

Do you want to create top secret messages that only your friends will be able to read? Here's how!

You will need:

- juice of 1 lemon • bowl
- plain paper • paintbrush
- heat source, such as a lamp or sunlight

1 Squeeze some lemon juice into a bowl.

2 Using the juice as ink, take a paintbrush and write a message onto a piece of paper.

3 Allow the paper to dry. The message will become invisible.

4 To read the invisible message, hold the paper to the heat source. If necessary, ask an adult to help you.

5 Lemon juice is mildly acidic and weakens paper. When the paper is heated, the acid turns the writing dark, so the message can now be read.

Got it?

Another way to read the message is to put salt on the drying ink. After a minute, wipe off the salt and color over the paper with a wax crayon. Your message will appear!

Top Secret

SPIES ON FILM

The glamorous and dangerous world of espionage is often portrayed in popular culture.

BOND, JAMES BOND

James Bond is probably the world's most famous spy. The fictional MI6 agent has appeared in a total of 14 books, including *Live and Let Die*, *The Spy Who Loved Me,* and *Moonraker*. Since Bond made his first appearance on the big screen in the 1962 film *Dr. No*, the Bond films have grossed billions of dollars worldwide!

IMPOSSIBLE HIT

Mission: Impossible started life as a popular 1960s TV series. Hollywood superstar Tom Cruise is the star of the *Mission: Impossible* films, which first hit theaters in 1996. Cruise plays agent Ethan Hunt, who leads an Impossible Missions Force, an unofficial branch of the CIA.

TEENAGE SPY!

Teen orphan Alex Rider stars in the *Stormbreaker* series of books by Anthony Horowitz. The first novel was published in 2000 and has been followed by a further eight titles, with more in the pipeline. The series follows Rider through his thrilling MI6 missions, an organization he joins when his uncle is killed in action. A *Stormbreaker* movie was released in 2006, and a TV series is on the way!

SECRET IDENTITY

Ex-CIA agent Jason Bourne is another character that started in books and has become a success on the big screen. Writer Robert Ludlum wrote the first Bourne novel, *The Bourne Identity*, in 1980. Jason Bourne is a highly trained undercover killer with no memory of his past life, fighting to regain his identity. Ludlum's first three books became a series of hit movies, with actor Matt Damon playing the mysterious agent Bourne.

The Bourne Identity, *The Bourne Supremacy*, and *The Bourne Ultimatum* have taken in more than $976 million at the box office.

SPIES AND DOUBLE AGENTS!

Spies usually operate undercover and stay out of the headlines. But sometimes they are caught. These are some of the most famous spies.

1. SPY TURNED TV STAR

Russian citizen Anna Vasilyevna Kushchyenko, also known as Anna Chapman *(below)*, was arrested in June 2010 in New York on suspicion of spying against the United States. Chapman and other members of her alleged spy ring pleaded guilty. They were sent back to Russia in July as part of a prisoner swap, with U.S. prisoners also released and sent home. Back in Russia, Chapman soon became a popular TV star with her own show and is even being tapped for future political success!

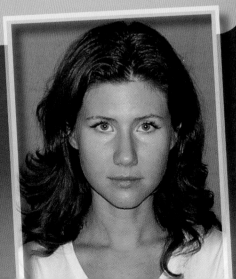

2. DANCING DOUBLE AGENT

From 1914 to 1918, Germany was fighting World War I against France and other countries. Legend says German officials persuaded exotic dancer Margaretha Zelle (stage name Mata Hari, *right*) to spy for them. She is supposed to have passed secrets from the important politicans and generals she danced for to her German spymasters. Legend also says she spied for France. When French officials found out about her spy activities for Germany, they put her on trial. She was found guilty and was shot by a firing squad in 1917. Later evidence suggested she was innocent.

3. SPOT THE BIRDY!

In Iran, suspicious government officials arrested two pigeons in 2008 for suspected spying! The story might not be as strange as it sounds. The pigeons were discovered close to one of the country's nuclear facilities. Iran's nuclear program has been an issue with the U.S. government, which believes that Iran is developing nuclear weapons. Iranian officials suspected the birds were carrying photographic equipment and had been trained to gather evidence!

4. POISONED TEA

Alexander Litvinenko escaped from Russia when Vladimir Putin came to power in the early 2000s. Litvinenko fled to London, England, and wrote two books accusing Putin and his supporters of terrorist acts. In November 2006, while at a restaurant, Litvinenko was poisoned when he drank tea laced with polonium-210, a highly toxic substance. He died three weeks later. To this day, no one has been brought to trial for his murder.

5. COLD WAR SPIES

Spies abounded during the Cold War. The Soviet KGB recruited many U.S. citizens in various walks of life. Some of the recruits, such as Julius and Ethel Rosenberg, had jobs that gave them access to important military plans and designs. Others, such as Aldrich Ames and Robert Hanssen, were highly placed U.S. agents. They caused the arrest and even deaths of their fellow agents by reporting them to the KGB. The Rosenbergs were tried and executed in 1953. Ames and Hanssen are serving life prison terms.

CIPHER WHEEL

Exchange secret messages with your friends using this amazing wheel to create spy codes.

You will need:

- pencil • pair of scissors
- tracing paper • card
- glue • cotter pin or brad

Cotter pin or brad

1

Trace the outer wheel *(shown right)*, including the text. On a separate sheet, trace the inner wheel. Glue the two tracings onto cards. Cut out both wheels. Make sure you do not cut off the black triangle on the smaller wheel.

2

Make a small hole in the middle of both wheels. Place the small wheel on top of the big wheel. Put the cotter pin through the holes. Bend up the ends of the pin so the two wheels stay together and turn.

3
Write down the message you want to send. For example, WE MEET AT MIDNIGHT. Make sure you destroy the message once you have made your code!

4
Choose a letter to be your key. In these instructions, we'll use the letter *H*. Turn the smaller wheel until the black triangle points to the key letter.

5
For each letter of your message, find that character on the outer wheel. Write down the letter that is below it on the smaller wheel. When you have finished, you'll have your coded message! This is the cipher:

WE MEET AT MIDNIGHT.
SP NPPR MR NLICLTAR.

Got it?

Your friend will need to make a cipher wheel too to decode your cipher. All your friend needs to know is the key, in this case the letter *H*.

STATS

20,000

The estimated number of CIA employees around the world

1776

The year that Nathan Hale, who is considered the first U.S. spy, was captured and killed by the British for espionage

17

The age of Belle Boyd when she began spying for the Confederate army during the Civil War (1861–1865)

2,000

The number of female special agents employed by the FBI

$7.9
BILLION

The FBI's annual budget

39
MILLION

The estimated number of spies in China—that's three percent of its population!

1953

The year Julius and Ethel Rosenberg were executed for passing U.S. secrets to the Soviet Union

1,271

The estimated number of U.S. government organizations working on counterterrorism, homeland security, and intelligence

GOING UNDERCOVER!

Further Reading

Earnest, Peter, and Suzanne Harper. *The Real Spy's Guide to Becoming a Spy*. New York: Abrams Books for Young Readers, 2009. Use this handbook to develop skills necessary to be a successful spy.

Fridell, Ron. *Spy Technology*. Minneapolis: Lerner Publications Company, 2007. This book describes the technology (both failed and successful) that spies have used throughout history to complete their missions.

Platt, Richard. *Spy*. New York: Dorling Kindersley, 2009. This illustrated resource gives an overview of the history, technology, and tools of espionage throughout history.

Shapiro, Stephen, and Tina Forrester. *Ultra Hush-Hush: Espionage and Special Missions*. Buffalo: Annick Press, 2003. Read this book for a collection of true tales of World War II espionage from both sides of the war.

Websites

CIA
http://www.cia.gov
Visit the Interactive Museum or Kids' Page to learn more about the functions of the CIA.

International Spy Museum
http://www.spymuseum.org/kidspy
Visit this website for games and information about the life of a spy.

National Security Agency
http://www.nsa.gov/kids/index.cfm
The NSA runs this site and tests kids on their ability to crack codes and puzzles.

Spy Secrets
http://www.topspysecrets.com
You are the spy, and at this website, you learn the techniques necessary for becoming a good one.

INDEX